Pam Muñoz Ryan

How Do You Raise a Raisin?

Illustrated by **Craig Brown**

Charlesbridge

To Virginia E. Ford, who was hungry for this book—Pam

For Mary, Beth, and Jane SPRINKLE, SPRINKLE—C.B.

How do you raise a raisin?

Tell me so I'll know.

They're such peculiar little things.

How do they sprout and grow?

Do raisins grow on Earth, or other planets, far away?

Do aliens collect them and space-shuttle them our way?

Raisins are dried grapes. So far, there is no proof
that raisins grow on other planets. Raisins ARE
grown on Earth, in countries like Turkey, Iran,
Greece, Australia, and the United States.

So, who discovered raisins?
Were they here when Earth began?
Who **WAS** the first to nibble them—dinosaur or man?

Raisins were probably discovered when someone or someTHING tasted grapes that had dried on the vine. Over the years people and animals figured out which grapes produced the sweetest, yummiest raisins.

Do raisins grow in **one** place,
like Raisin Creek or Raisin Hill?
Is there a special town called
Raisinfield or Raisinville?

Raisins grow best in areas with nice dirt, many days of hot weather, a dry climate, and plenty of water. Almost all of the raisins in the United States are grown in the San Joaquin Valley of California, near towns like Chowchilla, Dinuba, Kingsburg, Selma, Weedpatch, and even Raisin City! About 90 percent of the raisins sold in the United States come from the area around Fresno, California.

Raisinville, USA

Do farmers plant some seeds
from the local garden shop?
And wait for raisin bushes
to produce a raisin crop?

Farmers start a new crop of raisins by taking "cuttings"
from an older grapevine. These pieces of stem are planted
in sand until they sprout. Then, they are planted in the fields,
next to a wooden stake.

Notice how the grapevines
and the sprawling branches grow.
Does a grapevine tamer train them
into picture-perfect rows?

Grapevines are grown about eight feet apart. Fieldworkers hand-tie the sturdy branches, or "canes," to rows of wire. There are usually two sets of wire, a top set that is about six feet high, and a second wire that is three or four feet high.

How long do raisins take to grow?
A week, a month, or a year?
How many hours must you wait
for a raisin to appear?

It takes at least three years until the vines are old enough for the first crop of raisins. That's 26,280 hours!

When grapes are ripe and ready,
how do farmers get them down?
Do they rent a burly giant
to shake them to the ground?

When the grapes are ready, skilled grape-pickers snag the grape clusters from the vines using a sharp vine-cutter.

Most grapes are turned into raisins the same way they've been for thousands of years: they are left to dry naturally in the sun.

What do raisins lie on
while they're basking in the sun?
Do they rest on little beach towels
until they're dried and done?

The grape clusters are laid on brown paper trays on the ground between the grapevine rows. This is called "laying the grapes down." The sun rises in the east and sets in the west. Most raisin growers plant their vineyards in east-to-west rows. This way, grapes drying between the rows receive the most sun. If they were drying in north-to-south rows, the grapes would be in the shade part of the day, and when it comes to raising raisins, the more sun the better.

How long do clusters lie around
to sweeten, dry, and bake?
How many weeks in the valley heat
does raisin-making take?

Raisins bake in the sun for about two to three weeks. Then, the paper trays are rolled into bundles that look like burritos and are left in the field for a few more days to make sure that all the raisins are as dry.

Raisins do not look like grapes—
they're withered up and wrinkled!
Are they soaked inside a bathtub
until their skin is crinkled?

As grapes bake in the hot sun, their water evaporates. The more water they lose, the more the grapes shrivel, causing wrinkles.

How many grapes must a farmer dry upon the valley ground?
To make a box of raisins that weighs about one pound?

It takes about four and one-half pounds of fresh grapes to make one pound of raisins.

How do the raisins get from fields
to the raisin factory door?
Does a vacuum cleaner suck them up
from the dusty valley floor?

Farmworkers toss the raisin bundles into a wooden trailer. The raisins are sent across a shaker that gets rid of the dirt and rocks. Then, raisins are taken to the factory and stored in big boxes, called bins, until they are ready to be packaged.

Who puts raisins in the boxes
that keep them sweet and dried?
Do tiny fairy princesses
stuff each one inside?

When they're needed,
raisin bins are brought into
the factory for packaging. It takes
only 10 minutes from bin to package!
Workers and machines take off the stems and
capstems, sort, and wash the raisins. Then the
raisins are packaged in a variety of boxes and bags.

What happens to the raisins
that aren't the very best?
Are they sent to raisin prep school
until they pass the test?

When it comes to raisins, nothing is wasted! The stems and capstems are ground up and used for animal feed. Raisins that are not perfect are made into raisin concentrate that's used as a natural preservative in cakes, breads, and cookies. The best raisins are used for eating, baking, and adding to cereals.

Raisins taste so very sweet,
but they're considered "sugar-free."
Is each one dipped in a honey pot
by a busy honeybee?

Raisins are naturally sweet!

What's so great about raisins, anyway?

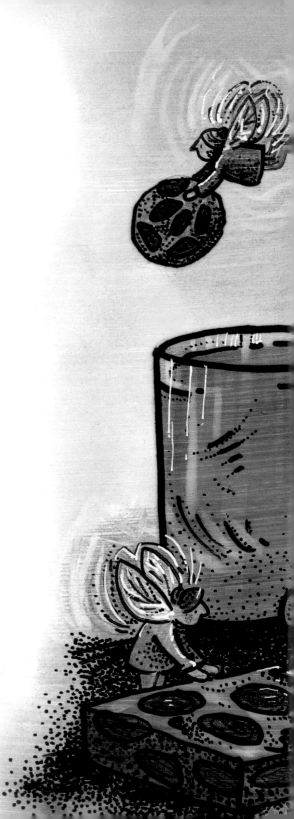

- They're nutritious. Raisins are rich in iron, calcium, potassium, and B vitamins and provide a good source of fiber.

- They make other foods taste better. Raisins have tartaric acid, a flavor-enhancer. Raisin juice and raisin paste are used in a variety of sauces such as pasta, barbecue, and steak sauces to boost their flavor.

- Raisin paste is sometimes used as filler in meatballs and meat pies to provide more servings.

- Raisins have a rich, natural color. Raisin juice is often added to frozen dairy desserts and baked goods as a color-enhancer, or food coloring.

- Ground raisins can be used instead of fat in fat-free baked goods like fat-free muffins, cookies, and brownies.

- Raisin paste and raisin juice concentrate are mold-inhibitors that prevent food from spoiling as easily. Bakers often use raisin products instead of artificial preservatives. Have you noticed that raisin bread lasts longer than other breads? Raisins extend the shelf life of bakery goods by several days over products without raisin products.

So, now you know how raisins grow.
Here's a little raisin history:

Between 1200–900 B.C., the ancient Phoenicians produced muscat raisins in Spain, so called because they were made from muscat grapes with their distinctive musk odor. The Phoenicians also made tiny raisins from small seedless grapes grown near Corinth, Greece. Called *raisin de Corauntz* by the French, they eventually became known as currants.

Hmmm, tangy and tasty.

Let's put them in the bread.

About the same time, Armenians grew a special seedless grape in Persia (Iraq, Iran, and Turkey). Historians say they were grown specifically for the rulers of the day, the sultans, so these raisins were called sultanas.

The early Greeks and Romans valued raisins so much that they were given as prizes in sporting events.

First Place! A parcel of raisins! What, no gold medal?

The Romans started using raisins in trade and the dried fruit became so valuable that they could be used to purchase just about anything.

Let's see, two pots of raisins, I can get a new toga, new sandals, and an arm bracelet for Mom.

Take nine raisins and call me in the morning.

I'm feeling a little old today, Doctor.

Doctors of ancient Rome and Greece began using raisins to treat all sorts of problems, from joint aches to old age.

The ancient general, Hannibal, who fought a war against Rome in the 200s B.C., fed raisins to his troops as they crossed the Alps.

Raisins didn't become popular in Europe until the 11th century when knights returning home from the Crusades brought raisins back with them from the Mediterranean and Persia.

Daddy, Daddy! Did you bring me a catapult?

No, son, but I brought you raisins.

Grape growing and raising raisins spread to France, Germany, and Spain. Then, in the 18th century, Spanish missionaries brought grape stock (pieces of grapevines) and the knowledge of grape growing (viticulture) to Mexico and what is now California.

Over the years, raising raisins flourished, but raisin seeds were a problem. When seeds were removed the raisins became a sticky, clumpy mess. Bakers and people who liked to eat raisins found this troublesome. They hoped for a seedless grape that would produce a yummy raisin.

In 1876, William Thompson introduced the Lady de Coverly grape to California. The green grapes were seedless, with thin skins, and produced a sweet and flavorful raisin. These grapes changed the raisin-producing industry forever and are still known today as Thompson Seedless grapes. Today 95 percent of the California raisin crop is Thompson Seedless grapes.

For centuries, from Hannibal to the astronauts, people have valued raisins. Scientists who planned the space shuttle menus knew that raisins are the perfect fast food for long journeys. They are lightweight, don't spoil easily, satisfy the craving for something sweet, and provide nutrition and energy.

Ants on a Log

Spread celery pieces with
    peanut butter, cream cheese,
    or cheese spread.
Top with raisins.

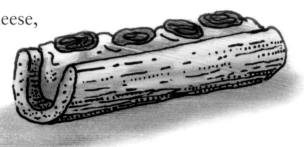

Rats on a Raft

Spread cream cheese on graham crackers.
Dot raisins on top.

Super Balls

1 cup honey
1 ½ cups powdered milk
1 cup peanut butter
1 ½ cups graham cracker crumbs
1 cup raisins
¾ cup crushed corn flakes or dried coconut

Put crushed corn flakes or coconut in a dish.
In a mixing bowl, mix all other ingredients.
Shape into balls.
Roll balls in crushed cornflakes or coconut.

The author wishes to thank the California Raisin Advisory Board, the Selma Chamber of Commerce, Sun-Maid Growers of California, the Serra Research Center of the Serra Cooperative Library System, the California Farm Bureau, Marla Woodcock, and the California Foundation for Agriculture in the Classroom.

Text copyright © 2003 by Pam Muñoz Ryan
Illustrations copyright © 2003 by Craig Brown

Published by Charlesbridge
85 Main Street
Watertown, MA 02472
(617) 926-0329
www.charlesbridge.com

Library of Congress Cataloging-in-Publication Data

Ryan, Pam Muñoz.
    How do you raise a raisin?/ Pam Muñoz Ryan;
illustrated by Craig Brown.
    p. cm.
    ISBN 1-57091-397-8 (reinforced for library use)
    ISBN 1-57091-398-6 (softcover)
    1. Raisins—Juvenile literature. [1. Raisins.]
I. Brown, Craig McFarland, ill. II. Title.
SB399.R93   2002
664'.8048—dc21   2001028263

Printed in South Korea
(hc) 10 9 8 7 6 5 4 3 2 1
(sc) 10 9 8 7 6 5 4 3 2 1

Illustrations done in marker and pastels
Display type and text type set in Catchup and Adobe Sabon
Color separations made by Sung In Printing, South Korea
Printed and bound by Sung In Printing, South Korea
Production supervision by Brian G. Walker
Designed by Diane M. Earley and Susan Sherman